VOCAL SELECTIONS

CAPTAIN LOUIE

MUSIC & LYRICS BY STEPHEN SCHWARTZ

Based on THE TRIP by Ezra Jack Keats

Book by Anthony Stein

Artwork by Ezra Jack Keats with special permission from the EJK Foundation.

ISBN 978-1-4234-8314-4

Williamson Music is a registered trademark of Imagem, C.V.

WILLIAMSON MUSIC®

A RODGERS AND HAMMERSTEIN COMPANY

EXCLUSIVELY DISTRIBUTED BY

HAL•LEONARD®
CORPORATION

7777 W. BLUEMOUND RD. P.O. BOX 13819 MILWAUKEE, WI 53213

Visit Hal Leonard Online at
www.halleonard.com

SYNOPSIS

Louie's family has recently moved to a new neighborhood. Lonely and feeling friendless ("New Kid in the Neighborhood"), Louie goes back to his room to play with his favorite toy, Red, his little red plane. When Red "suggests" they take a trip back to his old neighborhood, Louie makes a diorama out of an old shoebox covered with purple cellophane. He looks into it and, in his imagination, they are off! ("Big Red Plane")

As they fly towards the old neighborhood, sinister doings are afoot. A gang of oddly-shaped creatures—a Mouse, Monster, Sack, Broom, and Flower—are plotting to trick Louie when he arrives ("A Welcome for Louie").

Louie lands in his old neighborhood, but something is amiss. It's dark and empty. Louie calls out for his old friends, but the only answer is the echo of his voice. Suddenly, a whistle shrieks. Dark shapes jump out and chase Louie through the streets and alleys ("Shadows"). Louie is trapped, and the gang of creatures drags him to their hideout, where they give him the third degree. Just when it looks really bad for our hero, he notices, peeking out from the bottom of the "Sack," the tail of the neighborhood cat. These aren't frightening creatures at all. These are Louie's old friends dressed up for Halloween! After the trick is revealed, they all set out to celebrate Captain Louie's return ("Trick or Treat").

Louie and the Gang are joined by Julio. They are all about to set off for some trick-or-treating when one of the gang, Ziggy, mentions that someone has moved into Louie's old place. Indignant that anyone would dare to try to take Louie's place, they declare this new kid a LOOZA, and, led by Julio, they head off to "trick his house up good" ("Looza on the Block"). They are just about to launch their attack when they are surprised by Julio's mother exclaiming, "What is going on out there?" The gang stops dead in their tracks. It's Julio's house! Julio is the new kid! But he didn't want to admit it to his new friends.

Next, the Gang decides to go to Ziggy's house. They have never been there before because he lives in a scary neighborhood. Ziggy seems oddly resistant to the idea, but the gang insists. Ziggy is forced to admit that he didn't want his friends to go to his place because his family can't afford Halloween decorations and candy. Louie gets an idea and the gang heads off ("Spiffin' Up Ziggy's"). Halloween is almost over, so Louie suggests they go trick-or-treating by plane ("Captain Louie").

When they land, it is time for Louie to go. He bids his friends a warm farewell ("Home Again"), and he finds himself transported out of his diorama world and back into his new home. He hears his mother telling him to put on his costume and join the other kids, but he's just not sure. Then he remembers his old gang, and how Julio fit right in, and how he helped out Ziggy. He gathers up his courage, heads outside where, dressed as Captain Louie in his Red Plane, he makes new friends as the Halloween hit of his new neighborhood ("Finale").

—Anthony Stein, Book writer of *Captain Louie*

NEW KID IN THE NEIGHBORHOOD

Music and Lyrics by
STEPHEN SCHWARTZ

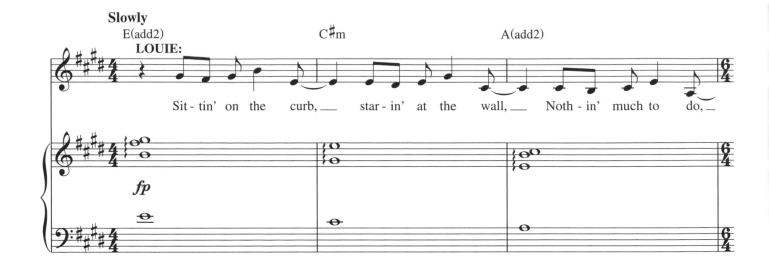

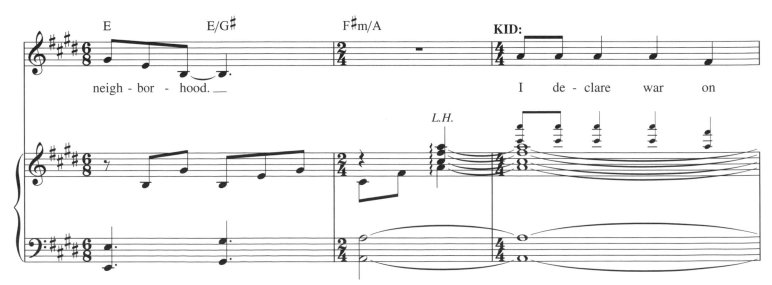

7

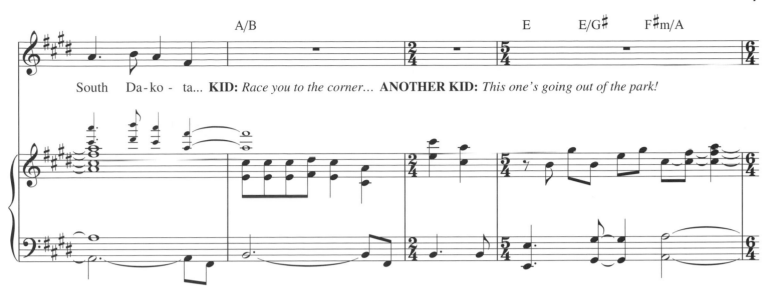

South Da-ko - ta... **KID:** *Race you to the corner...* **ANOTHER KID:** *This one's going out of the park!*

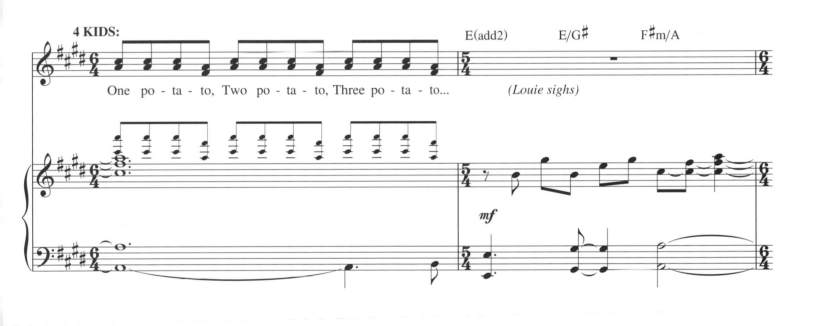

One po - ta - to, Two po - ta - to, Three po - ta - to... *(Louie sighs)*

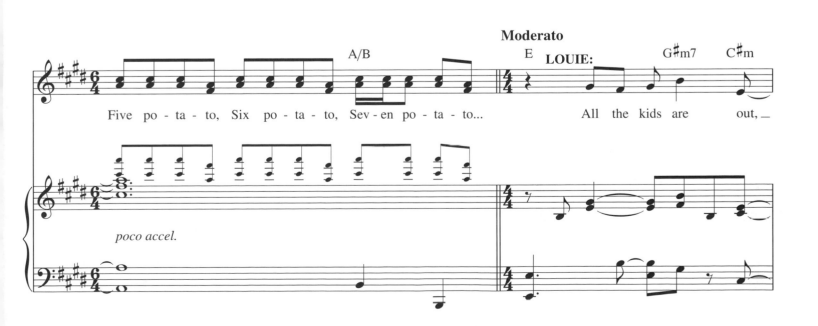

Five po - ta - to, Six po - ta - to, Sev-en po - ta - to... All the kids are out,

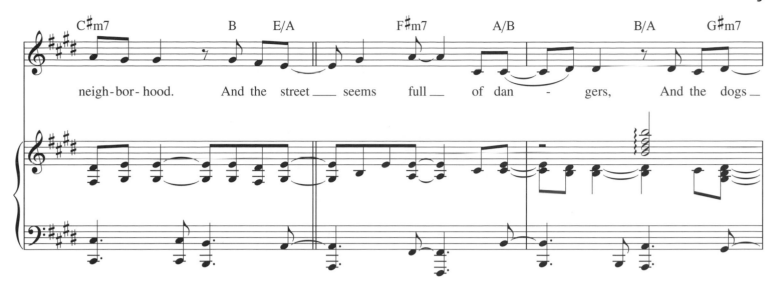

neigh-bor-hood. And the street ___ seems full ___ of dan - gers, And the dogs ___

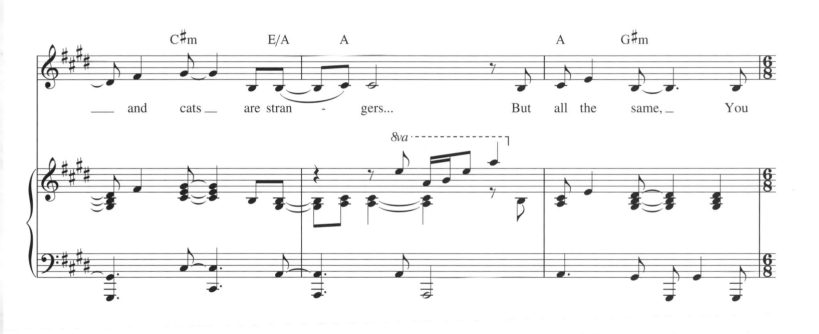

___ and cats ___ are stran - gers... But all the same, ___ You

wish you could run and join that game. _____

But they don't know your name, __ you don't know the score, __ All you know is

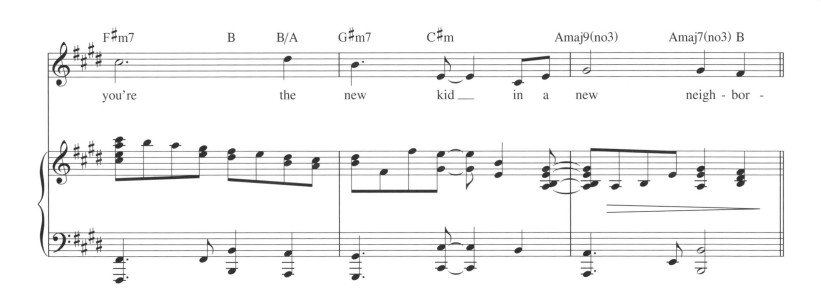

you're the new kid __ in a new neigh - bor -

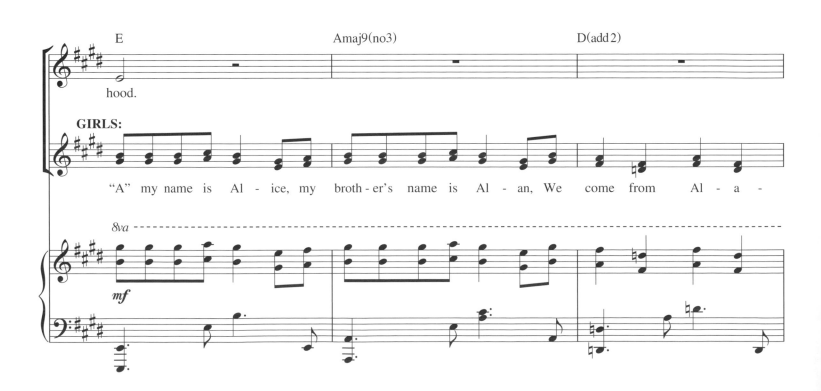

hood.

GIRLS:

"A" my name is Al - ice, my broth - er's name is Al - an, We come from Al - a -

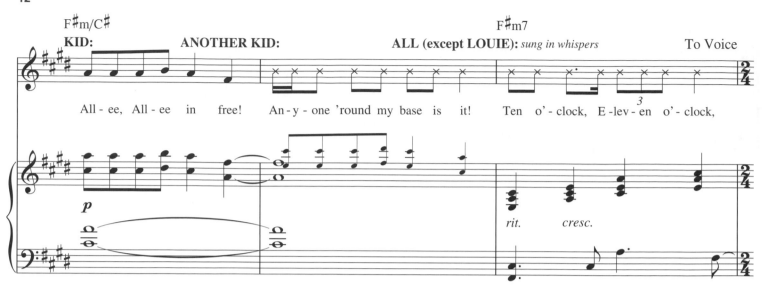

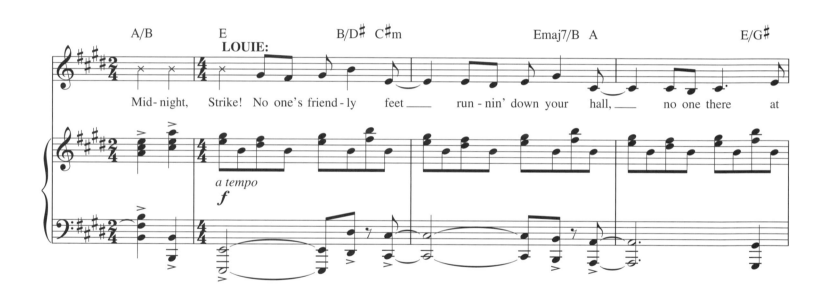

BIG RED PLANE

Music and Lyrics by
STEPHEN SCHWARTZ

* Cues are back-up vocals

16

* Solo or unison vocals

A WELCOME FOR LOUIE

Music and Lyrics by
STEPHEN SCHWARTZ

With menace

MOUSE: We got a wel-come for Lou - ie. Heh! Heh! Heh!
GANG MEMBERS: We got a wel-come for Lou - ie. Heh! Heh! Heh!

Slightly slower than "Big Red Plane"

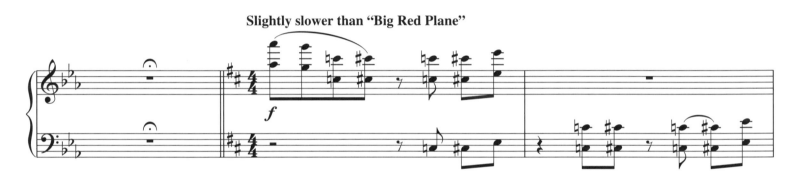

LOUIE: But if I,

GANG MEMBERS: We got a wel-come for Lou -

SHADOWS

Music and Lyrics by
STEPHEN SCHWARTZ

Lush Tango

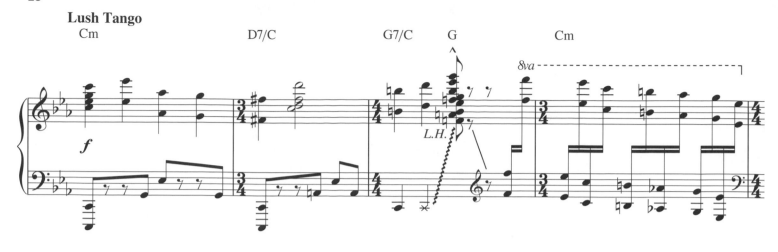

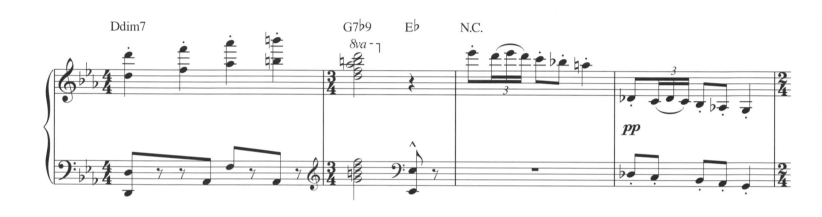

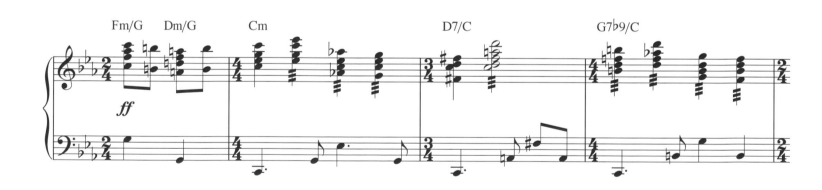

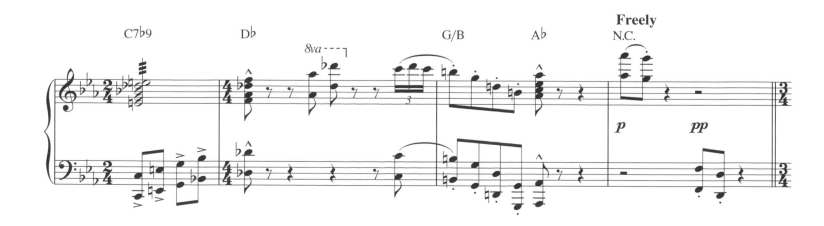

Quickly, like "chase" music

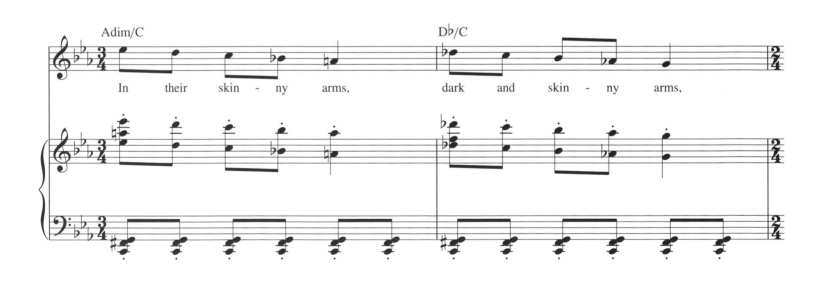

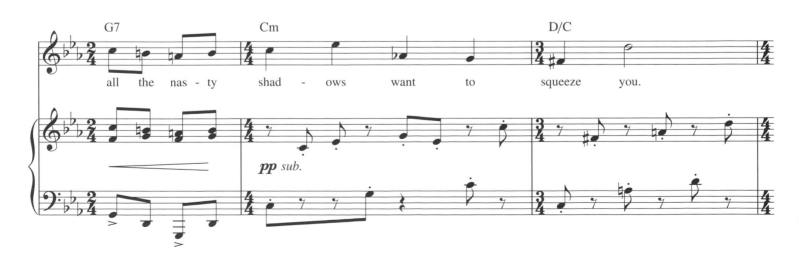

TRICK OR TREAT

Music and Lyrics by
STEPHEN SCHWARTZ

It's the night when the world goes cra-zy. When "Do your best" means "Do your

worst!" It's the night we wait for all year long.

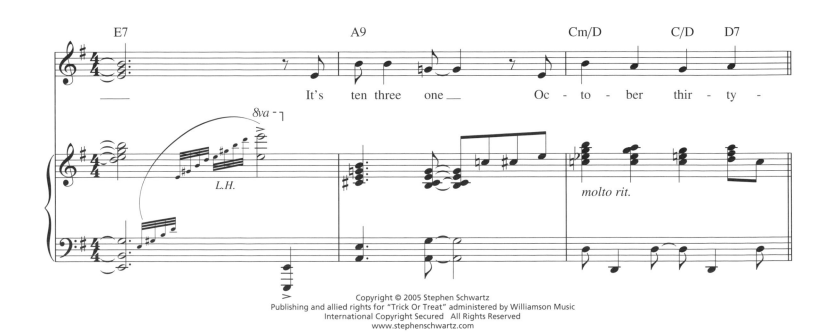

It's ten three one Oc-to-ber thir-ty-

34

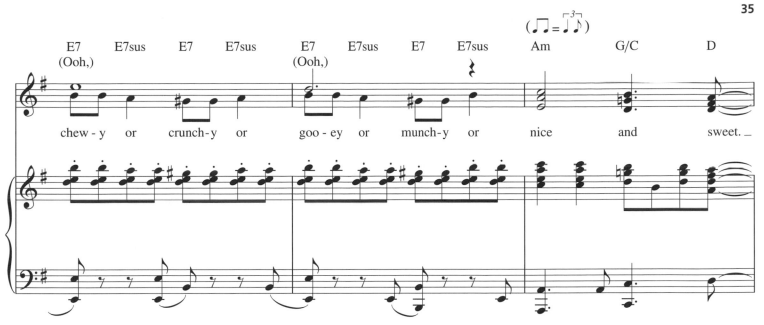

chew - y   or   crunch-y   or   goo - ey   or   munch-y   or   nice   and   sweet.

Trick   or _____   treat. _____

E. - T. and the Queen _

of Eng - land. Just look at the folks ___ you meet. ___

Bums and bun - nies and gyp - sy danc - ers. All come out ___ to

trick or treat! (Trick or treat!) Get your can ___ of shav -

Ba ba - ba - da ba - ba - da - da.

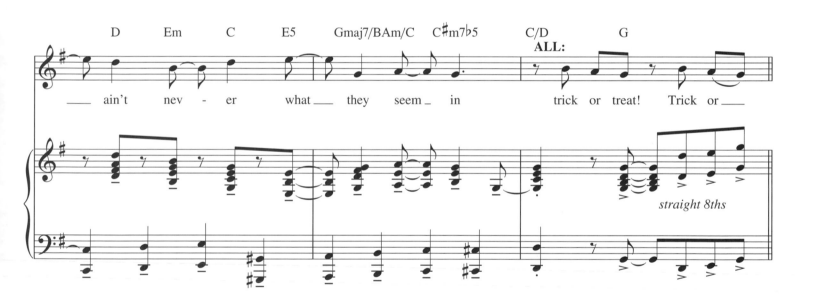

LOOZA ON THE BLOCK

Music and Lyrics by
STEPHEN SCHWARTZ

Medium Latin Rock

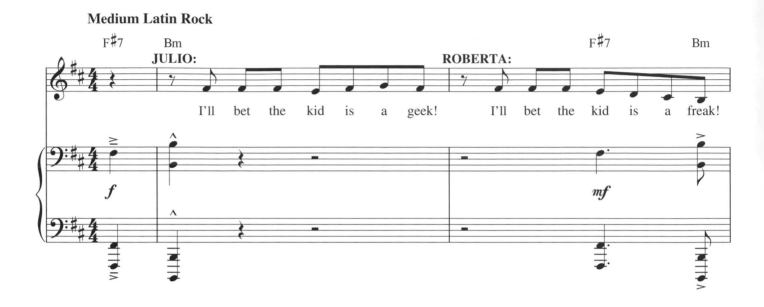

JULIO: I'll bet the kid is a geek! ROBERTA: I'll bet the kid is a freak!

ARCHIE: Looks like a thing that would sneak ___ from un - der a rock! ___ ALL: Oh, no! ___

We got a loo - za on the block!

42

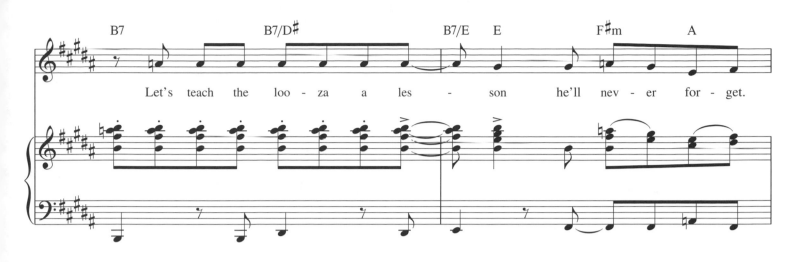

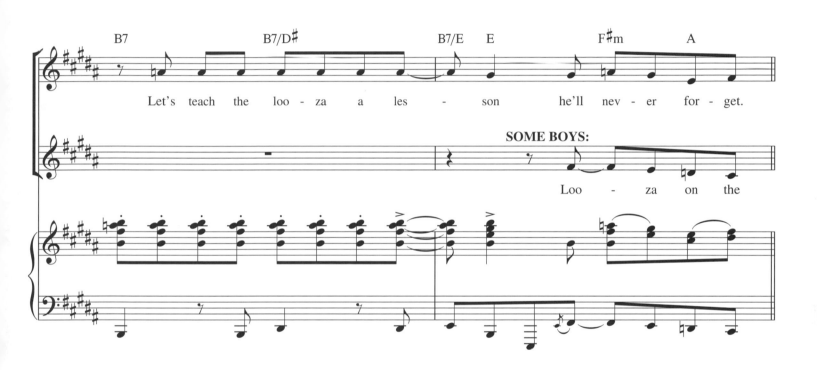

SPIFFIN' UP ZIGGY'S

Music and Lyrics by
STEPHEN SCHWARTZ

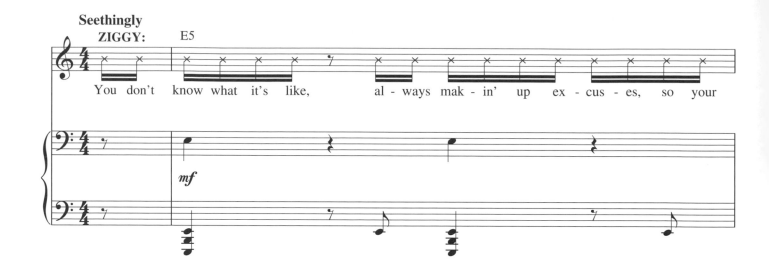

You don't know what it's like, al-ways mak-in' up ex-cus-es, so your

friends-'ll nev-er see where you live! You don't know what it's like won-d'rin' what-'ll I say this time?

What kind o' rea-son can I give? To-night at all your plac-es, you got jack-o'-lan-tern fac-es, you got

big bowls o' can-dy at your doors; But if you did-n't have e-nough so your place could have that stuff,

how would you feel a-bout yours? __ Al - right, so now you know. That's __ why you can't go! I been

keep - in' it in - side, but now you know. *Good! I hope you're satisfied!*

Funky, lightly swung 16ths

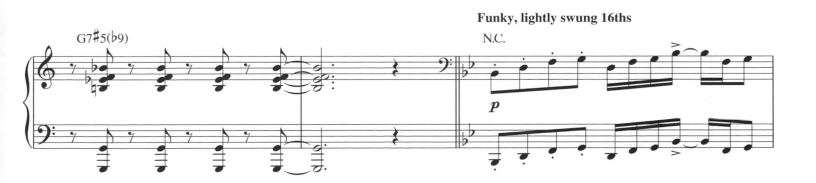

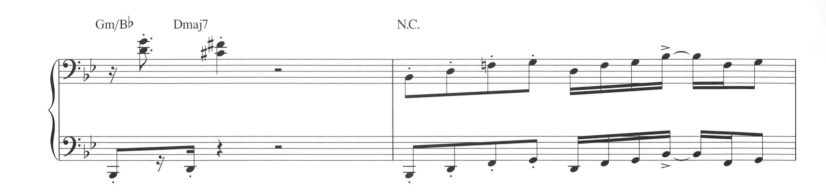

LOUIE: *We're going to use this to spiff up Ziggy's!*

LOUIE:

This   dead

CAPTAIN LOUIE

Music and Lyrics by
STEPHEN SCHWARTZ

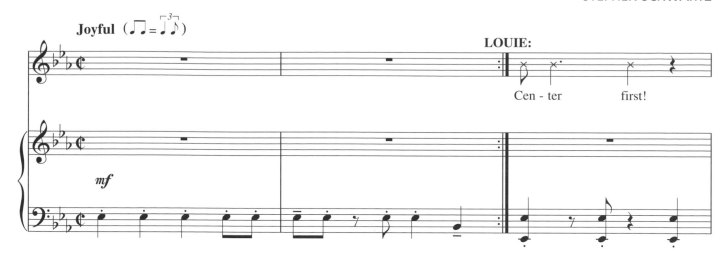

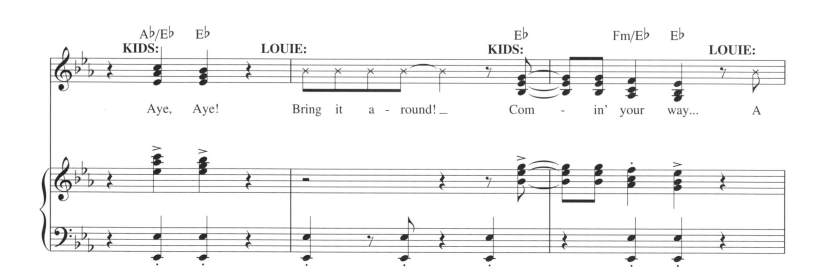

HOME AGAIN

Music and Lyrics by
STEPHEN SCHWARTZ

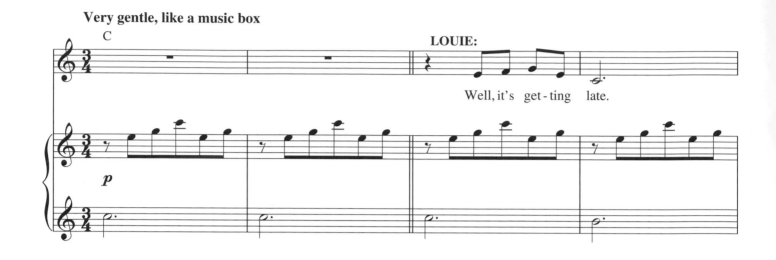

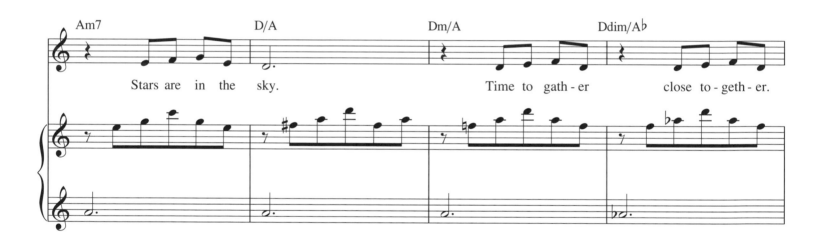

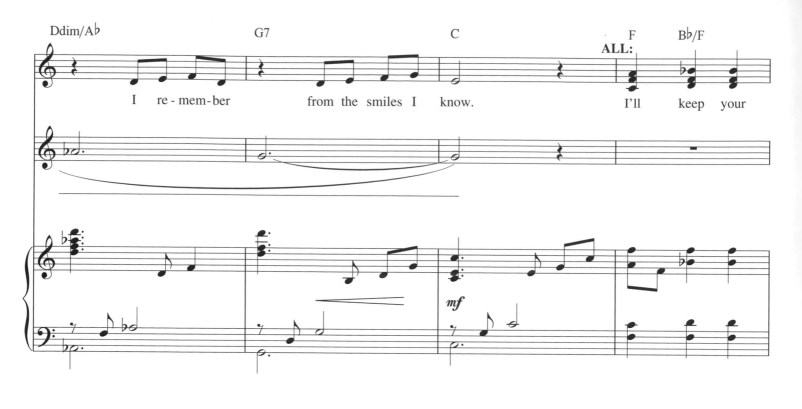

I re-mem-ber from the smiles I know. **ALL:** I'll keep your

smiles in - side me when I am

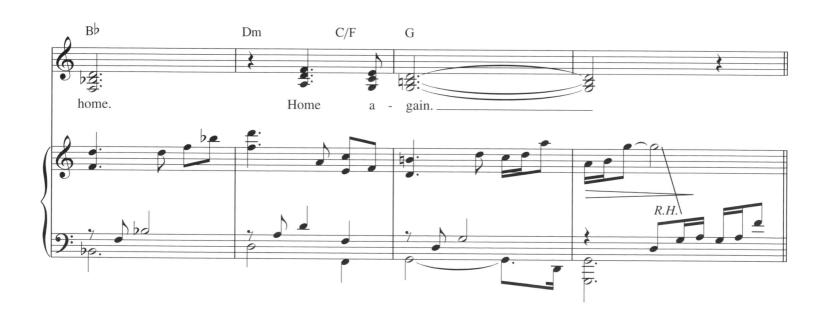

home. Home a - gain.

FINALE

Music and Lyrics by
STEPHEN SCHWARTZ

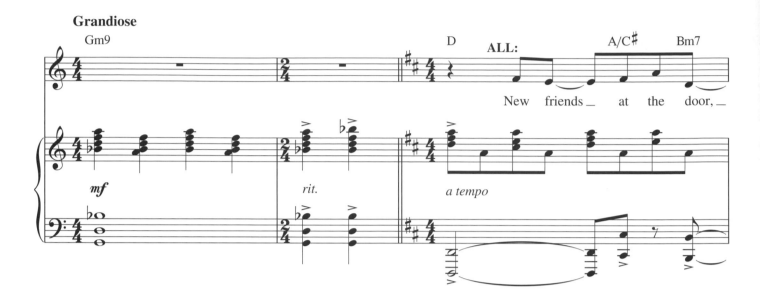

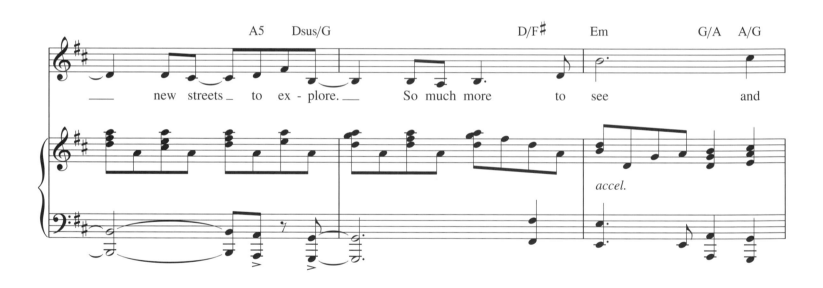